UNCOVERING THE PAST:
ANALYZING PRIMARY SOURCES

SEARCH FOR THE NORTHWEST PASSAGE

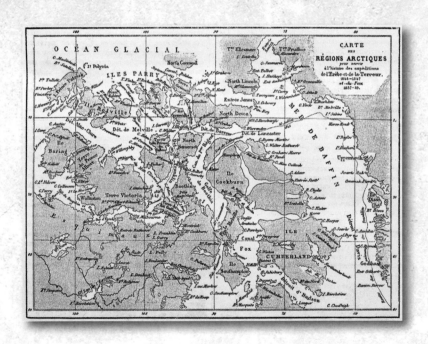

NATALIE HYDE

CRABTREE
PUBLISHING COMPANY
WWW.CRABTREEBOOKS.COM

Author: Natalie Hyde
Editor-in-Chief: Lionel Bender
Editors: Simon Adams, Ellen Rodger
Proofreaders: Laura Booth, Angela Kaelberer
Project coordinator: Petrice Custance
Design and photo research: Ben White
Production: Kim Richardson
Production coordinator and
  prepress technician: Ken Wright
Print coordinator: Katherine Berti
Consultant: Amie Wright,
  The New York Public Library

Produced for Crabtree Publishing Company
by Bender Richardson White

Photographs and reproductions:
Alamy: 18 (Science History Images), 19, 30 (Lebrecht Music and Arts Photo Library), 32 (John Mitchell), 37 (Chronicle); Getty Images: 8–9 (Pete Ryan), 31 (Mondadori Portfolio), 36 (Toronto Star), 40–41 (DigitalVision), 41 (Stringer); Cover illustration of Northwest Passage copyright © 2013 by Stan Rogers, Fogarty's Cove Music, illustrations copyright © 2013 by Matt James with cover design by Michael Solomon, reprinted by permission of Groundwood Books Limited15; Library and Archives Canada: 11, 23 Btm; Library of Congress: Top Left (Icon) 16, 18 (LC-DIG-ppmsc-02281), Top Left (Icon) 20, 22, 24, 26, 28, 30, 32 (LC-USZC4-11150); National Maritime Museum, Greenwich, London: 10–11; Princeton University Library: 24; Robert Harding: 38–39 (Egmont Strigl); Shutterstock: 3 (I. Pilon), Top Left (Icon) 4, 6 (Everett Historical), Top Left (Icon) 8, 10, 12, 14 (Marzolino), Top Left (Icon) 34, 36 (Evikka), Top Left (Icon) 38, 40 (AMFPhotography); Topfoto: 7, 12, 16–17, 22 (Topfoto), 6, 25, 33 Btm (The Granger Collection), 14, 23 Top, 27 (Topfoto/HIP), 20–21 (Roger-Viollet), 26 (World History Archive), 34–35 (Owen Beattie/University Alberta); Wikimedia.org: front cover
Map: Stefan Chabluk
Cover: (center) Lithograph of discovery of Franklin's boat on King William Island; (bgrd) Image of last handwrtten notes by members of Franklin's crew.

Library and Archives Canada Cataloguing in Publication

Hyde, Natalie, 1963-, author
    Search for the Northwest Passage / Natalie Hyde.

(Uncovering the past: analyzing primary sources)
Includes bibliographical references and index.
Issued in print and electronic formats.
ISBN 978-0-7787-4799-4 (hardcover).--
ISBN 978-0-7787-4818-2 (softcover).--
ISBN 978-1-4271-2088-5 (HTML)

    1. Northwest Passage--Discovery and exploration--History--Juvenile literature. 2. Northwest Passage--Discovery and exploration--History--Sources--Juvenile literature. I. Title.

G640.H93 2018   j910.9163'27   C2017-907713-9
                                         C2017-907714-7

Library of Congress Cataloging-in-Publication Data

Names: Hyde, Natalie, 1963- author.
Title: Search for the Northwest Passage / Natalie Hyde.
Description: New York, New York : Crabtree Publishing, 2017.
  Series: Uncovering the past: analyzing primary sources |
  Includes bibliographical references (p.) and index.
Identifiers: LCCN 2017057927 (print) | LCCN 2017059518 (ebook) |
  ISBN 9781427120885 (Electronic) |
  ISBN 9780778747994 (hardcover : alk. paper) |
  ISBN 9780778748182 (pbk. : alk. paper)
Subjects: LCSH: Northwest Passage--Discovery and
  exploration--Juvenile literature. | Arctic regions--Discovery
  and exploration--Juvenile literature. | Explorers--Northwest
  Passage--History--Juvenile literature. | Explorers--Arctic
  regions--History--Juvenile literature.
Classification: LCC G640 (ebook) | LCC G640 .H94 2017 (print) |
  DDC 910.9163/27--dc23
LC record available at https://lccn.loc.gov/2017057927

Crabtree Publishing Company

www.crabtreebooks.com   1-800-387-7650

Printed in the U.S.A./022018/CG20171220

Published in Canada
Crabtree Publishing
616 Welland Ave.
St. Catharines, ON
L2M 5V6

Published in the United States
Crabtree Publishing
PMB 59051
350 Fifth Avenue, 59th Floor
New York, NY 10118

Published in the United Kingdom
Crabtree Publishing
Maritime House
Basin Road North, Hove
BN41 1WR

Published in Australia
Crabtree Publishing
3 Charles Street
Coburg North
VIC, 3058

UNCOVERING THE PAST

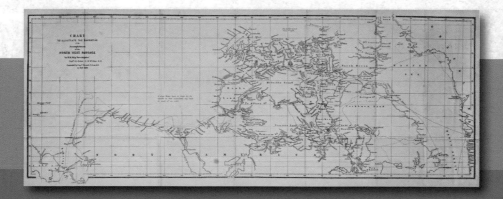

THE PAST COMES ALIVE

"History is for human self-knowledge ... the only clue to what man can do is what man has done. The value of history, then, is that it teaches us what man has done and thus what man is."

English historian R. G. Collingwood, 1946

In the 1800s parts of the world were still unexplored and unknown. These include large parts of the land, seas, and oceans of northern North America. Big blank spaces on maps showed where early mapmakers had yet to travel. Traveling the oceans wasn't just for exploration, though. Before cars and trucks were invented, much of the world's trade was done by sea. Safe, reliable water routes were **vital** for goods to be transported between countries and continents. The search for a sea passage through the Arctic, called the Northwest Passage, lasted for several hundred years and involved men from nations from all over Europe. It is a story of human **tragedy,** failure, and disaster. It is also one of determination, **endurance,** and courage.

Studying past events, such as the search for the Northwest Passage, is important to understand the present. By looking back in time we see what drove people to find solutions or answers to problems that existed. New scientific theories were tested. New technologies were invented. We see how trade, wealth, and the desire for power launched exploration of vast and dangerous territories. We learn from the tragedies and failures of the past. We have to know where we've come from as a people to know where we're headed.

▶ **Willem Barents was a Dutch navigator who sailed in search of a northeast passage across the Arctic in the late 1500s.**

Northwest Passage: A sea route connecting the Atlantic and Pacific oceans through the Canadian Arctic

Arctic: The north polar region consisting of the Arctic Ocean, neighboring seas, and parts of Alaska and northern Canada

Expedition: A journey by a group of people for exploration or scientific research

Exploration: Traveling in a new area in order to learn about it

Scientific revolution: A new way of thinking about science and technology

EVIDENCE RECORD CARD

Willem Barents's ship in the Arctic ice

LEVEL Secondary source
MATERIAL Colored woodcut
LOCATION Barents Sea
DATE 1598
SOURCE Topfoto

LOOKING AT HISTORICAL EVIDENCE

The search for the Northwest Passage happened long ago in a **remote** area. So how do we find out about the people who participated, what they thought, what they lived through, and the **Indigenous peoples** and places affected by their actions? We can look back at historical **evidence.** Evidence is the result of our actions. If we write something down, paint a picture, or tell a story, we are creating a trail that other people can study. By studying the items created both at the time and after the event, we can begin to understand what happened.

The amount of evidence that exists for an event depends on many factors. Sometimes the event happened so long ago that there is no written record. Evidence that might be seen as a **security risk** could be destroyed or kept hidden. Natural disasters can wipe out stored records. On the other hand, events that were important worldwide, such as missions to the International Space

▼ An Inuit family travels across the sea ice to their fishing camp near Bathurst Inlet, Nunavut. They use a dog-pulled **sledge** for transportation, as did some explorers of the Northwest Passage.

PERSPECTIVES

What details in this photograph show you that the family is well-prepared for life in the Arctic? Where do you think they learned these skills? Do you think this territory is their **permanent** home?

Station, would create a large evidence record. Projects supported or developed by a government usually leave large amounts of documents and images as part of its reporting and record system.

The beginning of the search for the Northwest Passage happened before photography, the Internet, video recordings, and even the telephone. But there is still a lot of evidence because governments of several countries were involved as they encouraged explorers to find a new trade route.

A **historian** is someone who studies a particular event, person, or time frame in the past. Historians interested in the search for the Northwest Passage can focus on one specific expedition, such as **English** Captain Luke Foxe's of 1635, or specific area of exploration, such as Frobisher Bay, or the effects on the Inuit people. With the search taking several hundred years, involving several different countries, there are many historians dealing with this subject. In this book, we discuss their work and observations.

NORTH-VVEST FOX.

OR,

Fox *from the* North-west *passage*.

BEGINNING

With King ARTHVR, MALGA, OCTHVR, the two ZENIS of *Iseland*, *Estotiland*, and *Dorgia*; Following with briefe Abstracts of the Voyages of *Cabot*, *Frobisher*, *Davis*, *Waymouth*, *Knight*, *Hudson*, *Button*, *Gibbons*, *Bylot*, *Baffin*, *Hawkridge*. Together with the Courses, Distance, Latitudes, Longitudes, Variations, Depths of Seas, Sets of Tydes, Currents, Races, and over-Falls; with other Observations, Accidents and remarkable things, as our Miseries and sufferings.

Mr. IAMES HALL's three Voyages to *Groynland*, with a Topographicall description of the Countries, the Salvages lives and Treacheries, how our Men have beene slayne by them there, with the Commodities of all those parts; whereby the Marchant may have Trade, and the Mariner Imployment.

Demonstrated in a Polar Card, wherein are all the Maines, Seas, and Ilands, herein mentioned.

With the Author his owne Voyage, being the XVIth, with the opinions and Collections of the most famous Mathematicians, and Cosmographers; with a Probabilitie to prove the same by Marine Remonstrations, compared by the Ebbing and Flowing of the Sea, experimented with places of our owne Coast.

By Captaine LVKE FOXE of Kingstone *vpon* Hull, Capt. and Pylot for the Voyage, in his Majesties Pinnace the CHARLES.

Printed by his Majesties Command.

LONDON,
Printed by B. ALSOP and THO. FAVVCET, dwelling in *Grubstreet*, 1635.

▶ The first page of Captain Luke Foxe's book about his search for a northwest passage. It includes sections on the expeditions of other explorers such as John Cabot and Martin Frobisher.

"The white men were very thin, hollow-cheeked, and looked ill. They were dressed in white man's clothes, had no dogs, and were traveling with sledges which they drew themselves. They bought seal meat and blubber, and paid with a knife. There was great joy on both sides at this bargain, and the white men cooked the meat at once with the aid of the blubber, and ate it."

Testimony in 1923 of Iggiararjuk, an Inuit, about his father meeting Sir John Franklin (see pages 24–25)

TYPES OF EVIDENCE

"Knowledge is power. Information is liberating."

Kofi Annan, Secretary-General of the United Nations, 1997

Evidence left behind from the past is called source material. Source material can be created by humans, such as the pyramids, the Empire State Building, or a memorial to World War II. It can be a product of nature such as dinosaur fossils. Source material can be created **deliberately** or by accident. Indigenous people drew pictographs on rock walls to celebrate their **culture** and history. Ammunition left behind from rifles of soldiers fighting in the War of 1812 was forgotten after the war. The source material from the many expeditions into the Canadian Arctic was a combination of all these things. Shipwrecks, grave sites, reports, and ice mummies all contribute to our understanding of the importance and dangers of the search for the Northwest Passage.

Without source material, events in the past would be lost from our memories and records. Without seeing mistakes to learn from, or successes to copy, it is impossible for **society** to improve and move forward. The first maps that were created from Arctic expeditions show just how unknown that region of the world was at that time. Entire areas of the maps are blank and on some of the maps islands are shown that explorers assumed were there under the ice, but are in fact nonexistent.

Source material can be found in museums, **archives,** libraries, and even private collections. Government images and reports are carefully stored. Newspapers and photographs might be lost or forgotten in attics or basements. Conservators work hard to restore and preserve source material so it is available for future generations to study.

▼ Over time, wind, ice, and cold temperatures break down wooden structures, such as this building on Beechey Island, Nunavut, Canada, where three graves of **British** explorer Sir John Franklin's crew are found.

ANALYZE THIS

Do you think that source material left in the Arctic would be **preserved**? Why or why not? Do the snow and ice help any types of material survive over time?

PRIMARY SOURCES

Source material can be sorted into primary, secondary, and even **tertiary sources.** Each one has a role to play in our understanding of the past. **Primary sources** are firsthand accounts or direct evidence of an event. They can be written material, such as **transcripts** and diaries. **Visual** primary source items are images, such as photographs and maps, and **auditory** primary sources are things you can hear, such as interview recordings.

Written primary sources can take many forms:

- Diaries and Journals: Books in which people document their personal thoughts and events, usually every day
- Newspapers: Papers reporting on daily events, locally, nationally, or internationally
- Advertisements: A card or a flyer or space in a newspaper or magazine to offer something for sale or rent
- Transcripts: Written copies of the text of speeches, meetings, and recordings
- Letters: Documents sent between people
- Telegrams: Coded messages sent over long distances using wire signals that are decoded and written down
- Lyrics: Words to songs that people sing
- Blogs: Journals posted on the Internet
- Social media: Websites where people post messages, images, and videos

There is a strong trail of primary written sources for the search for the Northwest Passage. The idea of a new trade route would have been big news at the time. There are lots of newspaper articles in libraries and

> *"Strangely enough the thing in Sir John's narrative that appealed to me most strongly was the sufferings he and his men endured. A strong ambition burned within me to endure those same sufferings."*
>
> Roald Amundsen on reading as a child Sir John Franklin's accounts of his Arctic explorations

ARTIFACTS AS PRIMARY EVIDENCE

Artifacts are items that are made by humans and left behind as evidence. Artifacts were very important in piecing together what happened to some men who lost their lives in the Arctic. Tin cans, pieces of pipes, muskets, and shoes help us understand what daily life was for sailors. Copper nails and parts of ships can help scientists locate shipwrecks.

▶ Artifacts from Sir John Franklin's last expedition in **1845**, including a tinned can of food, give an insight into his crew's daily life.

Mr. SAM
late Chief at
Hu

Published as the Act d

archives. Large expeditions, such as those traveling from Europe to the Canadian Arctic, needed funding for large crews and supplies. Governments were usually the source of the money. They required explorers to create and deliver written reports and travel logs.

In the time before telephones, letters were the most common way to communicate. Letters from the explorers to their families about how they were dealing with the excitement and fear of sailing into the unknown are a rich source of information. So, too, are the diaries, journals, and log books of sea captains. They give an insight into the search and day-to-day life aboard ship.

▲ From 1769 to 1772 English explorer Samuel Hearne traveled overland from the East Coast to the Arctic to try to find a northwest passage. His writings are the most detailed description of the life of northern Indigenous peoples from that time.

VISUAL AND AUDITORY EVIDENCE

Primary source images are packed with information. They can bring out emotions in the viewer such as sympathy, horror, and curiosity. Photographs can be filled with details that would take pages of notes to match. Paintings can highlight differences in society and cultures not only by what subjects the artists include, but also what they leave out.

Visual primary sources can include:

- Maps: Diagrams that show the features of a certain area of land
- Paintings: Images made by an artist on canvas with paint
- Photographs: Images created using a camera that are printed on paper or stored **digitally**
- Political cartoons: Illustrations or comic strips with a political message
- Posters: Large printed images with pictures and words, often an announcement
- Billboards: Large outdoor advertisements
- Movies, films, and videos: Moving images recorded by a camera and projected on screens

▼ English explorer Sir Martin Frobisher's meetings with the Inuit in 1576 started out friendly, but then mistrust grew when five members of his crew went ashore and didn't return. On his next expeditions in 1577 and 1578, his crew was armed and battled with the Inuit.

Some of the most important visual materials to be created during the search for the Northwest Passage are maps. Much of the **mainland** shore and the Arctic islands were encased in ice most of the year. Travel to and through this area was extremely challenging. With such a long distance to go to reach the area and then a very short period of warm weather, it took many years and several different expeditions to accurately map the entire area. The first expeditions were taken before cameras were invented, and later expeditions didn't always take photographers and their heavy, bulky equipment with them. Paintings and sketches were created to give people back in Europe an idea of this **exotic** landscape and the unfamiliar Inuit who lived there.

Audio primary source material, such as songs and sheet music, are another type of evidence. Songs created around the time of explorations give another **perspective** on people and events. "Lady Franklin's Lament" is a folk song with lyrics written just five years after Franklin left on his last voyage. It gives an idea of the anguish Lady Franklin must have felt when her husband disappeared.

PERSPECTIVES

Apart from drawing a map, what other useful information seen here might these Inuit have given Ross and his crew about the Arctic? What primary evidence is shown in the illustration?

▼ John Ross, a Scottish explorer, had friendly relations with the Inuit he met. This illustration from his journal of 1832 shows them aboard his ship, *Victory*, drawing him a map of the area.

▲ British author Charles Turley wrote many biographies of sea captains such as Robert Scott, Fridtjof Nansen, and, of course, Roald Amundsen, who found the Northwest Passage (see pages 30–31).

SECONDARY SOURCES

Secondary sources are evidence material one step away and separate from the actual event. Secondary sources are usually created by studying or evaluating the information found in primary source material. Just like primary sources, secondary sources can be written, visual, or auditory. Textbooks, novels, magazines, histories, encyclopedias, and poems are examples of written secondary sources. Movies and songs written about past events are visual and auditory examples. Indexes or information compiled from secondary and primary sources are called tertiary source material. Tertiary sources are not usually used for research, but rather are a way to find primary or secondary sources.

Other secondary sources include:
■ Maps: Modern-day diagrams that show historical information
■ Websites: Internet pages that feature information about situations and events
■ Interviews: Discussions with subject-matter experts who did not directly experience the situation or event
■ Documentaries: Movies or television and radio programs based on factual events. These may include primary source material.

"... a musket shot or shotgun blast has a distinctive sound, even from a mile away, and sound travels almost supernaturally far and clearly this far north— but it's true that the ice pack squeezing ever more tightly against [the ship] Terror is always rumbling, moaning, cracking, snapping, roaring, or screaming."

Dan Simmons, *The Terror*

The mystery and fascination with the search for the Northwest Passage has been documented in many published books. Nonfiction, such as *Across the Top of the World* by James Delgado and *Northwest Passage* by Matt James, and fiction like *The Terror* by Dan Simmons, are just a few of the many books on the subject. Magazine articles from the 1870s focused on massive icebergs and the **heroics** of the explorers. Poems, such as Gwendolyn MacEwen's "Terror and Erebus" or Brandon Humphreys's "Northwest Passage," give readers a taste of adventure of the search.

Movies are considered secondary sources because the plot and characters are based on what we know of the facts, but also change some details to create entertainment.

Secondary sources are valuable to historians when they act as a summary of a vast amount of primary sources. They are also helpful when primary sources are in a foreign language and research is based on a **translation**. They can also give us a new perspective on events. Novels and movies allow people to reflect on things that happened in the past and see them through the eyes of someone else.

ANALYZE THIS

Some books, movies, and poems about the Northwest Passage try to capture the emotions of the search. What primary sources would be best for an insight into how it felt to explore the high Arctic?

NORTHWEST PASSAGE

STAN ROGERS

AS SEEN BY MATT JAMES

▶ This book uses the lyrics of the 1981 song "Northwest Passage" by Canadian musician Stan Rogers to retell and illustrate the story of the search for this mysterious route.

INTERPRETATION

"It is in literature that the greater truths about a people and their past are found."

Writer F. Sionil José, born 1924

Historians who are studying source material are careful to remember that it was made in the past when society had different knowledge, beliefs, and values. These differences shape people's **interpretation** of facts, which is known as **bias**. Bias is reflected in how and what source material is created and its conclusions. Historians deal with bias by considering The Bias Rule, which states:

- All material must be looked at **critically.**
- The creator's point of view must be considered.
- Each piece should be compared with other sources.

What evidence of bias might people notice when looking at sources from the search for the Northwest Passage? During the height of the period of exploration, at about the 1840s, Europeans were eager to expand their territories and "claim" land they considered empty. Artifacts, such as English flags and crosses bearing the French coat of arms, were placed along the route in an attempt to claim and expand those countries' empires. In some documents, explorers gave English names to places, plants, and animals, ignoring the Indigenous peoples' names for them. In European explorers' diaries, the Inuit are seen as savages. George Best, who documented Martin Frobisher's voyage, told of the captain's demand to capture one of them. Frobisher referred to the captive as his men's "praye" (prey). This also explains why, in their official papers and reports, Europeans never mention asking permission from the Inuit for free passage through their native land.

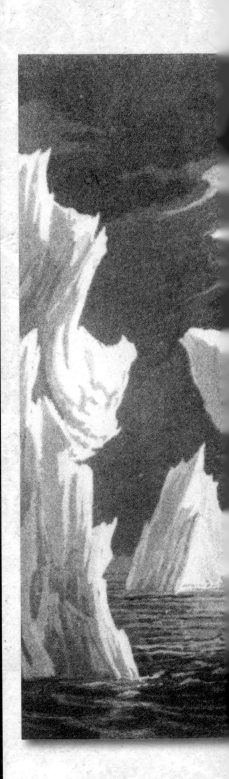

This image shows John Ross's perspective of the Arctic. How do you think he felt about his journey? What feeling do you get from the shapes and colors he used? Looking at the ships, how difficult and dangerous do you think the journey must have been?

EVIDENCE RECORD CARD

John Ross's search for the Northwest Passage in ships including his *Isabella*

LEVEL Primary source

MATERIAL Book illustration

LOCATION Near Baffin Bay

CREATOR Sir John Ross and printmaker Robert Havell

DATE February 1819

SOURCE British Library

▲ This watercolor illustration is from John Ross's *A Voyage of Discovery*. It shows his expedition sailing through the ice formations in the Arctic.

ANALYZING BIAS

Historians have to be aware of other factors while researching a person, place, or event. While still keeping bias in mind, they use the Time and Place Rule to **evaluate** source material. This rule states that the closer in time to the actual event the material is created, the more likely it is that the information is accurate. Here is a list of sources ranging from those that are most preferred by historians to those less preferred:

- Direct traces of an event, such as a flag left at a discovery site or a ruined building
- Material created at the time the event happened, such as photographs, a ship captain's log book, or a sketch or map of a battlefield
- Material created after an event by firsthand witnesses or participants, such as a sailor's **correspondence**

- Material created after an event by people who use interviews or evidence from the past, such as a newspaper report or a police officer's witness report made with a victim of a crime

The setting in which an event happens must also be taken into consideration when considering its historical value. The setting and time frame is called the **context**. The context can influence why an event happened or why people acted in a certain way. The search for the Northwest Passage happened at a time when wealthy people in Europe wanted

▼ John Ross's illustration from his journal of 1818 of meeting the Inuit for the first time. These Inuit of Baffin Island had never before seen Europeans. Both sides traded small items and shared their culture and lifestyle as best they could without speaking each other's language.

▲ This is John Ross's illustration of Hibluna, an Inuit woman. She is shown doing a dance of delight upon being given a metal cutting tool, and she is also holding a local bone knife.

exotic items from the East. However, it took many week or months for goods and spices to be transported from Asia to Europe. What was needed was an easy and faster trade route. Rival trading companies, such as the Dutch and the English East India Company, were competing for rights to trade with a certain area. This would ensure that they would make large profits.

This was also a time of expanding overseas territories and empires. Explorers and adventurers were hired by monarchs to find a way through the ice and northern islands of the Arctic. A new route would open up new areas for European countries to claim and **colonize**.

Readers and researchers need to be aware of this context when reading documents written in the time period of any historical event.

PERSPECTIVES

Look closely at how John Ross drew the Inuit in his journal illustrations. How did he **portray** them? What are their facial expressions and gestures? Do you think he enjoyed meeting them? What details in the images support your answer?

"If the proposed Expedition should unfortunately not be entirely successful in effecting a passage, it must contribute to our Geographical knowledge; and it cannot fail to make important additions to the series of Magnetical observations which are now carrying on in every part of the world."

Excerpt from letter from Sir John Franklin to Admiral Lord Haddington

SEARCHING FOR A WAY

"Her Majesty's Government having deemed it expedient that further attempt should be made for the accomplishment of a north-west passage by sea from the Atlantic to the Pacific Ocean."

Lord Haddington, Leader of the British Admiralty, letter to explorer John Franklin, May 1845

ANALYZE THIS

Do you think the risk and cost to European countries of sending expeditions into the dangerous Arctic of North America and the loss of life was worth finding a shorter route to Asia? Why or why not? Are expeditions to the Moon and perhaps Mars comparable?

When Marco Polo returned to Europe from the East in 1295 with spices and silk, Europeans became eager to establish trade with this exotic region. Overland routes to and from Asia were long and difficult, so Europe's leaders knew they had to find a quicker, safer route by sea.

The first voyage into the uncharted northern seas was made by Italian explorer John Cabot. England's King Henry VII granted him "**letters patent**," which gave him permission to sail into areas not claimed by Spain or Portugal. Cabot reached Canada's east coast in 1497 but did not sail far into the Arctic.

France was next to send someone. Jacques Cartier set sail in 1534. His route took him to the coast of Newfoundland and then around the northern peninsula to the Gaspé region. He sailed down the St. Lawrence River thinking this mighty river might cut right through the continent. He didn't find the Northwest Passage, but he claimed land for France along the St. Lawrence and set up fur trading there.

This started a string of new expeditions. England's Martin Frobisher made three expeditions and reached what is now called Frobisher Bay. (See map on page 43.) Englishman John Davis also made three expeditions starting in 1585. Davis Strait is named after him. On his third attempt, Englishman Henry Hudson reached Hudson Bay in 1611, and wintered in James Bay. He wanted to continue, but his crew set him adrift in a boat. He was never seen again.

▼ Early Arctic explorers had to prepare to spend more than a year on their journey. The sea ice would quickly encase ships and leave crews stranded for months.

EVIDENCE RECORD CARD

Norwegian Roald Admunsen's ship the *Gjøa* fights its way through sea ice

LEVEL Primary source
MATERIAL Black-and-white photograph
LOCATION Northwest Passage, Canadian Arctic
DATE 1904
SOURCE Topfoto Images

ROSS'S AND PARRY'S VOYAGES

By the 1800s the search for the Northwest Passage had also become a scientific and **geographic** project. In 1818 John Ross was given the command of the Arctic expedition to solve the question of a sea route. He was aboard the *Isabella* while another English explorer, Sir William Edward Parry, was on the *Alexander*. Both ships headed north and west around Baffin Island and into Lancaster Sound. As Ross sailed into the sound, he thought he saw mountains at the other end of the strait and named them the Croker Mountains. He decided there was no exit, turned back, and returned to England. Parry disagreed.

In 1819 Parry went back to the Arctic with the *Hecla* and *Griper* and instructions to investigate Lancaster Sound. As he sailed farther west he proved that the Croker Mountains didn't exist. He continued on through Barrow Strait until he was near Melville Island. The ships became trapped in ice, and Parry prepared to spend the winter there. The ships were not free of the ice until the following August, when Parry pushed farther west. Near Cape Dundas, Parry realized that they could go no farther that season and turned back for England. But his journey was a success

ANALYZE THIS

What types of information did William Baffin include on his map of his Arctic voyage? How useful would you find this map if you had to use it to sail into the unknown territory?

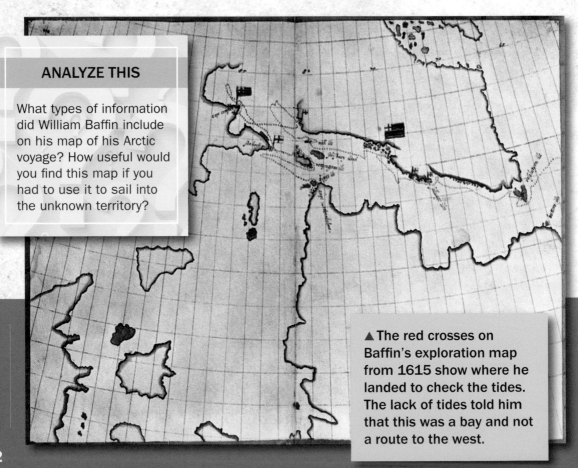

▲ The red crosses on Baffin's exploration map from 1615 show where he landed to check the tides. The lack of tides told him that this was a bay and not a route to the west.

in that he had proven that Lancaster Sound opened up a passage to the west and also revealed the existence of many islands. Parry was also the first to prove that it was possible for ships and their crews to spend the winter in the Arctic.

According to Parry's journal, he took special care to keep the men warm and dry. Food was rationed so it would last. The men drank lime juice and sugar in water each day to prevent **scurvy**. To keep the morale up for the men, Parry had the men put on plays and also prepare a weekly newspaper. As the ice broke up, Parry's journal told how the ships made their way back toward England and of the Inuit they met, who were eager to trade with them.

GRAPHIC ILLUSTRATIONS OF ANIMALS.
SHEWING THEIR UTILITY TO MAN, IN THEIR SERVICES DURING LIFE AND USES AFTER DEATH.

Published by THOMAS VARTY, 31 Strand, London

THE SEAL AND WALRUS.

◀ This illustration is from a book about animals published in 1845. Around the center image of the seal and walrus are examples of how these animals were hunted and used. The images on the right relate to the Hudson's Bay Company which traded animal furs.

▲ A fur trading scene from "A Map of the Inhabited Part of Canada from the French Surveys," 1777.

"To be prepared against the chances of meeting with any natives in the countries … the ships were directed to be furnished with a large quantity of various kinds of presents, both to secure their friendship and to purchase any supplies of which we might stand in need."

Sir William Edward Parry, Journal of a Voyage for the Discovery of a North-West Passage From the Atlantic to the Pacific, 1819-20

FRANKLIN'S FAILED ATTEMPT, 1845

John Franklin's first journey into the Canadian Arctic was not by sea but by land. He had hoped to map the northern shoreline and coast to figure out if a passage was possible. In May 1819 he sailed to York Factory, Manitoba, and then on to Cumberland House, Saskatchewan. From there he tried to explore the north on snowshoes. He was short of supplies, men, and equipment. Eleven crew members died of starvation and injuries on the journey back to the nearest fort. Franklin vowed to be better prepared the next time.

His second expedition, 1825–1827, was much more successful. Traveling north from the United States, he and his crew split into two groups. Franklin explored the coastline to the west in a boat. The others explored to the east. When they returned to England, they had mapped 370 miles (595 km) of **uncharted** coast.

It took 20 years before the government would pay for another attempt to find the Northwest Passage. In 1845 Franklin

▼ This map shows the discoveries British explorers made from 1818 to 1826. The expeditions of Sir James Ross, Sir John Franklin, and Sir William Edward Parry helped to map the rivers and coastline of the Arctic.

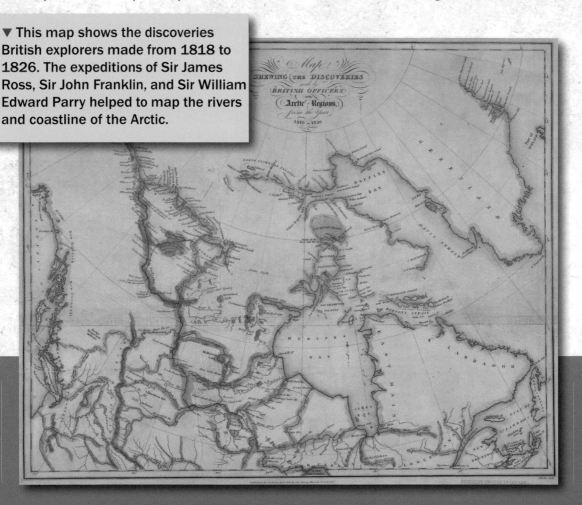

▲ After Franklin's death, his crew tried to walk to safety. They pulled a lifeboat full of supplies behind them. But the cold and lack of food was too much for them to survive. This 1895 painting shows artist W. Thomas Smith's idea of the crew's last days before the men died.

set sail again. This time he took two ships, the *Terror* and the *Erebus*. He stocked the ships with a new invention—tin canned food. He took enough food for three years. He knew he would likely be caught in the winter ice before making it all the way through. He didn't want to face starvation again.

Two whaling ships saw the *Terror* and *Erebus* in late July 1845 in Baffin Bay. Franklin was waiting for good weather to continue on into Lancaster Sound. It was the last time anyone heard from him and his crew or saw them alive. Evidence shows they spent the winter of 1845/1846 on Beechey Island. During that time three men died and were buried there. In September 1846 the ships sailed on but were trapped in sea ice near King William Island. After two years of not hearing from her husband, Lady Franklin called for a search party. No one knew what had happened to the ships or the crew.

ANALYZE THIS

All the supplies John Franklin's crew needed had to be brought with them. What sort of evidence might they have left behind for searchers to find? Would all the evidence be intact over many years? If not, what might happen to it?

"The Ships are now complete with supplies of every kind for three years: they are therefore very deep — but happily we have no reason to expect much Ice as we proceed farther."

Sir John Franklin, Whale Fish Islands, July 12, 1845

McCLINTOCK'S SEARCH

The first news that Franklin's crew had died came from Scottish explorer John Rae, who was in the Arctic mapping the coastline. He had great respect for the Inuit living there and had a good relationship with them. He learned that the Inuit had seen white men in the Arctic hauling a boat, planning on heading south. Later the Inuit found the men's dead bodies, and they also had artifacts including a silver plate engraved with Franklin's name on it.

Lady Franklin was frustrated with the British government's attempts to find her husband. Many expeditions had returned with no information. She hired Sir Francis McClintock who set sail on the *Fox*. He found the graves of three crew members on Beechey Island, and an Inuit woman told him the rest of the crew had starved to death. He also found the crew's last written report in a stone **cairn** on King William Island. McClintock brought the sad news back to Lady Franklin. In 1859, he published *The Voyage of the "Fox" in the Arctic Seas: A Narrative of the Discovery of the Fate of Sir John Franklin and His Companions*.

Pressure in Britain to know what happened convinced its government to send Robert McClure in the *Investigator* and Richard Collinson in the *Enterprise* in 1850 to search from the western

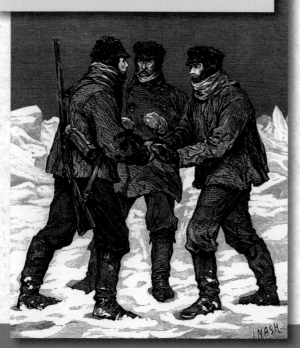

▼ Knowing how many men had died in the Arctic, Robert McClure was relieved to meet up with Lieutenant Pim and his crewmate of the HMS *Resolute*.

ANALYZE THIS

Lady Franklin had to hire her own ship and crew to look for her husband. Why do you think the British government was not in a hurry to look for Franklin?

"April 25, 1848 - H.M. ships 'Terror' and 'Erebus' were deserted on the 22nd April, 5 leagues N.N.W. of this, having been beset since 12th September, 1846. The officers and crews, consisting of 105 souls, under the command of Captain F.R.M. Crozier, landed here in lat. 69° 37' 42" N., long. 98° 41' W. Sir John Franklin died on the 11th June, 1847; and the total loss by deaths in the expedition has been to this date 9 officers and 15 men."

Sir Francis Leopold McClintock, *The Voyage of the 'Fox' in the Arctic Seas: A Narrative of the Discovery of the Fate of Sir John Franklin and His Companions.*

entrance near Point Barrow, Alaska. The *Investigator* sailed ahead of the *Enterprise* but got as far as Victoria Island before becoming trapped in ice in September. On October 21, McClure wrote in his log that he had seen Melville Island, which was the other end of the Northwest Passage. They made some progress over the next summer when the ice released its grip, but were stuck again in Mercy Bay the following fall.

McClure's ship was frozen in place all that winter and the next summer, too. His team was forced to abandon the *Investigator* in 1853 and use sledges to make its way to the *Resolute,* a ship from another expedition that had sailed in search of them and anchored off Melville Island. Collinson's team had completed the Northwest Passage from west to east but not entirely by ship.

PERSPECTIVES

This painting was created before the passage had been found and conquered. It has the subtitle, "It might be done and England should do it." Why do you think the painter used an old sailor in the picture? Do you think the sailor felt confident that the Northwest Passage would be found and conquered? What gives you that impression?

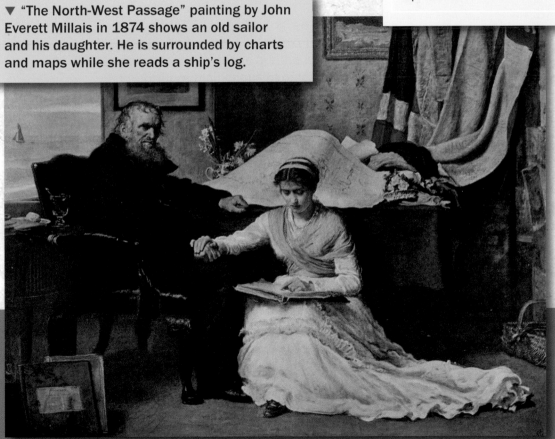

▼ "The North-West Passage" painting by John Everett Millais in 1874 shows an old sailor and his daughter. He is surrounded by charts and maps while she reads a ship's log.

OTTO SVERDRUP CHARTS THE EAST

After the disastrous Franklin expedition and the difficulties of the other attempts at crossing the Northwest Passage, interest in the route by trading companies faded. People realized that the short summers and dangerous ice would make the passage unreliable. However, large sections of the Arctic were still unmapped and unexplored.

Otto Sverdrup was a Norwegian sailor and Arctic explorer. In 1902 he sailed up the coast of Greenland and then headed west into uncharted territory. He and his small crew spent three years wintering on Ellesmere Island. He also discovered and mapped three more islands now called the Sverdrup Islands. He had a different approach to traveling and doing research in the cold north. He learned from and **adopted** Inuit ways. He wore Inuit-style fur clothing to stay warm and used their methods of hunting and fishing. This allowed him to stay and chart 100,400 square miles (260,035 sq km). While he didn't find a northwest passage, he did confirm that there was no route north of Lancaster or Melville sounds.

When Sverdrup returned to Oslo in 1902, he claimed the Sverdrup Islands for Norway. The Canadian government

> "Just as we were arranging the procession for the march upon the ice, five female narwhals suddenly appeared, and immediately afterwards a small seal was seen in the lane abreast of the ship—an enlivening sight, which we accepted as a good omen for the coming summer."
>
> Otto Sverdrup—excerpt from *Farthest North: Vol II.*

ANALYZE THIS

Why do you think Otto Sverdrup and his crew were successful in staying in the Arctic for three years when other earlier expeditions were fatal for some or all of their crew?

argued that all islands in the Canadian Arctic, whether mapped or not, were Canadian. Finally an agreement was reached in 1930. Norway let go of their claim. The Canadian government agreed to buy Sverdrup's records of his expeditions. Today, copies of Sverdrup's maps and his records that were left behind buried in cairns in the Arctic are part of the holdings of the National Archives in Ottawa.

◀ The *Fram* was the ship Otto Sverdrup used in exploring the Arctic region. It was built for polar exploration, with a rounded bottom that could escape being trapped in ice.

▼ Otto Sverdrup published a book in Norwegian about his Arctic journey in 1903. The next year it was translated into English and is an important primary source of information of his scientific expedition.

AMUNDSEN COMPLETES THE ROUTE

Expeditions had mapped the northern coastline of Canada and most of the islands. The Northwest Passage had been found but a challenge still existed—to cross the passage entirely by ship.

That is not what Roald Amundsen of Norway had in mind when he set out in 1903, though. His plan was to find the magnetic North Pole. It is the spot on Earth to which compass needles point north. Its location can move because of changes in Earth's core. Amundsen wanted to see if the exact spot had moved since it had been found in 1831.

Amundsen started out in his shallow fishing boat, *Gjøa,* and a crew of only six men. He wanted to keep a small and **tight-knit** group who would be kept busy. It was also easier to live off the land with fewer men. The first season he made it south of King William Island and could see open water to the west. He would have been able to cross from east to west in one season if he had continued. But Amundsen decided to overwinter in a harbor he called Gjøahavn (Gjøa Harbor). Over the winter he met with a small band of Netsiliks Inuit. He and his crew learned how to make igloos, make their sledge runners work in low temperatures, and how to keep warm with animal skins. The Norwegians gave the Inuit knives, needles, and matches. They earned each other's respect. Amundsen stayed two years in the harbor, taking magnetic readings and living among the Netsiliks.

In the spring of 1905 the crew made ready to continue westward. Four days after starting they reached Cambridge Bay. On August 26, 1905, they met with the *Charles Hanson,* a whaling ship. The captain congratulated Amundsen on being the first to complete the Northwest Passage by ship. In his diary, Amundsen wrote, "The Northwest Passage was done. My boyhood dream— at that moment it was accomplished."

▶ The *Gjøa* follows a steamboat into San Francisco Bay having sailed through the Northwest Passage.

3030 Norwegian Sloop Gjøa. Captain Amundsen entering San Francisco Bay
FIRST VESSEL TO PASS THROUGH THE N.W. PASSAGE

▲ Norwegian explorer Roald Amundsen (second from right at back) poses on the deck of his ship, *Gjøa*, with his crew in 1906.

ANALYZE THIS

Do you think Amundsen's diary is an important primary source about Arctic exploration? What sort of **unique** information might you find in his writings?

"All the Eskimos [Inuits] went hunting this morning. I accompanied them. Walking into a biting wind is not enjoyable. My hunting companion noticed that my nose was turning white, so he sat down to remove one of his own kneewarmers which he stretched over my nose. That was helpful. He was cold, but less than me."

Diary of Amundsen, March 24, 1904

LARSEN MAKES IT, THERE AND BACK

It took until the 1940s for the second crossing of the Northwest Passage. This time it was accomplished by a Canadian. Henry Larsen was born in Norway, but immigrated and became a British citizen in Canada in 1927. Like his hero, Roald Amundsen, he wanted to explore the Arctic. In 1928 he got his wish when he was **commissioned** to the Royal Canadian Mounted Police (RCMP) schooner, *St. Roch*. Its job was to take supplies to the RCMP posts all across the Arctic.

▼ The RCMPV St. Roch was a Royal Canadian Mounted Police schooner. It was the first sailing ship to completely sail around North America, including through the Northwest Passage under Henry Larsen.

In June 1940, after 12 years of patrolling the north, the RCMPV *St. Roch* left Vancouver, British Columbia, to head west to east through the Northwest Passage. Larsen ran into trouble with sea ice so decided to overwinter at Walker Bay, Northwest Territories, near the entrance to the Prince of Wales Strait. In the summer of 1941 the ice broke up and Larsen was able to sail through to Gjøa Haven, where Amundsen had overwintered. He pushed forward and by September took shelter on the west side of the Boothia Peninsula. The next summer he pushed through the ice and made it to the Hudson's Bay Company post in Fort Ross, Nunavut. He sailed down the eastern coast of Canada and arrived in Halifax in October 1942. In 1944

Larsen made the difficult crossing again. This time he crossed east to west, like Amundsen had done. Larsen made it in only one season.

Some primary source documents point to the idea that Larsen's journey through the passage had another purpose. His journey was made during the time of World War II (1939–1945) and reports mention the plan for Larsen to land in Greenland and secure it for the **Allies**. This would prevent foreign enemies from using it as a base to attack North America. This never happened, but the evidence shows that perhaps Larsen and his crew were doing more for Canadian Arctic **sovereignty** than just supplying RCMP posts.

▲ The Inuit gave Henry Larsen the name Hanorie Umiarjuag, which means "Henry with the Big Ship."

▼ Matthew Henson was the first African-American Arctic explorer. Here with some of the crew on the quest to the North Pole, left to right: Donald MacMillan, George Borup, Capt. Bob Bartlett, and Matthew Henson.

A LOST EXPEDITION

"Our work truly felt like a forensic investigation of a modern mass disaster—but it actually occurred in a previous century."

Dr. Owen Beattie, anthropologist, University of Alberta

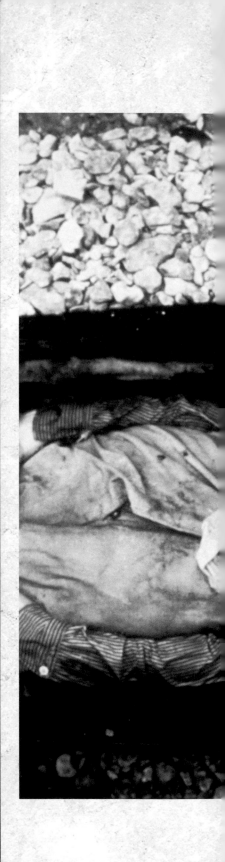

For more than 100 years, the fate of Franklin's two ships and all the crew was a mystery. Stories from the Inuit were full of terrible tales. Did the crew really turn to **cannibalism?** How did the three crew members buried on Beechey Island die? What happened to those who were left? Scientists turned to primary evidence for answers.

In 1984, Dr. Owen Beattie, an anthropologist from the University of Alberta, Canada, **exhumed** the bodies of the three men buried on Beechey Island. After analyzing skin and hair samples, he discovered that the men had dangerous levels of lead in their bodies. He believed that it came from the tinned food they had on the ships. One of the symptoms of lead poisoning is poor thinking ability. This might explain some of the strange decisions the crew made. Instead of staying by the ships, they tried to pull heavy sleds and walk hundreds of miles (km) south.

Another important source of information about Franklin was the report found by Lieutenant William Hobson of the *Fox* in a stone cairn. The report stated that in 1847 Sir John Franklin was commanding and "All well." But around the edges of the document, another message was added later to report that by April 1848 the ships had been deserted, and 24 men had died, including Captain Franklin. Examinations of a leg bone found on King William Island and reports from the Inuit who had witnessed some of crew showed that the remaining crew had turned to cannibalism to try to survive.

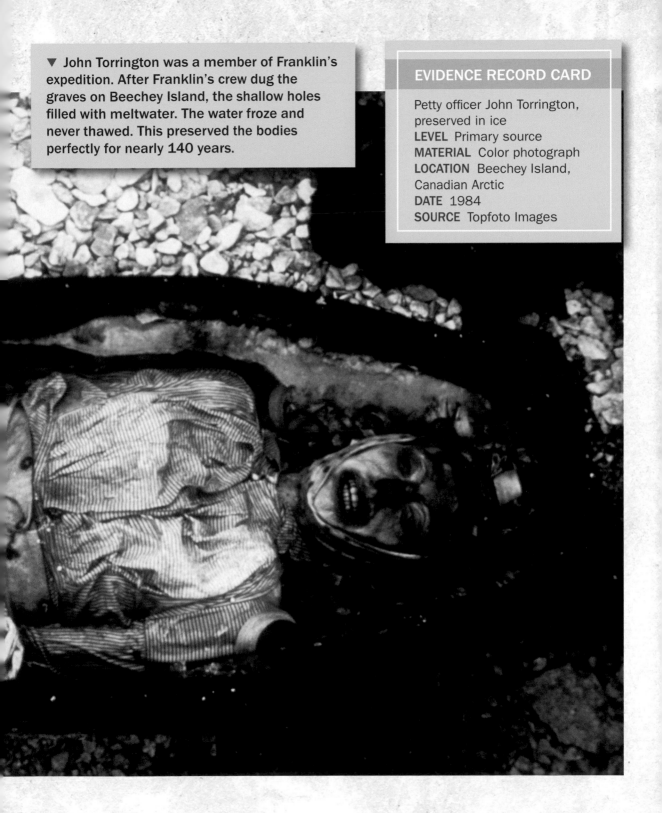

▼ John Torrington was a member of Franklin's expedition. After Franklin's crew dug the graves on Beechey Island, the shallow holes filled with meltwater. The water froze and never thawed. This preserved the bodies perfectly for nearly 140 years.

EVIDENCE RECORD CARD

Petty officer John Torrington, preserved in ice
LEVEL Primary source
MATERIAL Color photograph
LOCATION Beechey Island, Canadian Arctic
DATE 1984
SOURCE Topfoto Images

HUNTING FOR FRANKLIN

Source material was also **vital** as scientists worked to find Franklin's sunken ships, the *Terror* and the *Erebus*. The ships had already been named a national historic site by Canada even though they hadn't yet been found. The Canadian government was also eager to establish sovereignty in the region. The search was a great way to bring attention to and gain some national pride in the Arctic and its history.

Researchers used two sources of information. One was primary source material created from new scientific devices. Side-scan sonar sends out sound waves to make images of the sea floor. These can show artifacts or entire ships sitting on the bottom of the ocean. The search of the suspected location helped to map the seafloor in a large area of the Arctic around King William Island. The other vital link in the search for the ships was the use of oral histories of the Inuit. Some of the interviews with the Inuit are primary sources, such as news from hunters who saw ships' masts sticking out of the ice. Others are secondary sources, such as family stories of ancestors who saw Franklin's crew or

ANALYZE THIS

Why do you think it was important to find Franklin's ships, the *Terror* and the *Erebus*? What artifacts might still remain after all this time? What information might researchers gain from studying the wrecks?

"*The idea was, if we find Inuit archaeological sites where they had lots of material from these ships, that might suggest those sites are located near where one of the ships was, it might give us a better idea where the ships ended up when they actually sank.*"

Robert Park, archaeologist, University of Waterloo

▲ **Archaeologists** with Parks Canada began searching for Franklin's two ships, the HMS *Terror* and the HMS *Erebus* in 2008.

the remains of their camps.

The first abandoned ship found in the Arctic wasn't one of Franklin's ships at all. In 2010, searchers found the HMS *Investigator*, which had been sent in 1848 to find Franklin's ships. It was found in Mercy Bay where Inuit oral history said it would be. The search continued for Franklin's ships with a **collaboration** between Parks Canada, the Canadian government, and several museums, universities, and trading companies. Researchers turned to local Inuit again. They heard the information passed down in communities and saw artifacts collected long ago at the sites. The team found the *Erebus* in 2014 and the *Terror* in 2016 using a combination of modern science and indigenous history.

PERSPECTIVES

Look closely at this image of the record found on King William Island. What factors might make it difficult to read? What can a researcher do to make sure any transcription of it is accurate?

EVIDENCE RECORD CARD

Naval form from Franklin's expedition found on King William Island

LEVEL Primary source
MATERIAL Paper document
LOCATION National Maritime Museum, London, England
DATE 1847
SOURCE Collections Royal Museums, Greenwich, England

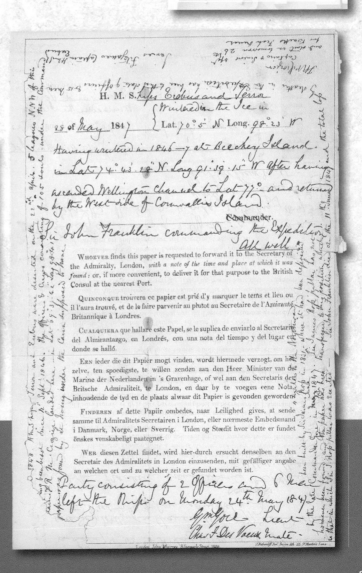

▶ Details on the form showed where the ships had been. Investigators used data about ice floes and currents to figure out where the shipwrecks might have drifted.

HISTORY REVISITED

"The Arctic is among the highest priorities for this government."

Andree-Lyne Halle, speaking for Prime Minister Justin Trudeau

For hundreds of years the thick, shifting ice in the Arctic made the Northwest Passage almost **impassable** and very dangerous. Even after a route was found and successfully navigated, the short season of open water kept the route from being commercially worthwhile. In 2016, there were only 16 successful complete voyages through the passage.

Now, climate change is opening up the Arctic and making the route more reliable. Also, technology has changed since the explorers risked their lives to make the journey. Today, goods can be shipped between Europe and Asia in many different ways. There are ocean liners and trains to carry **freight** across seas and continents quickly and safely. Airplanes can move freight around the world in hours instead of months. The Panama Canal that links the Atlantic and Pacific oceans means ship traffic can cut about 8,000 miles (12,875 km) off their trip.

The melting ice has also allowed more exploration and scientific study in the Arctic. CHARS is the Canadian High Arctic Research Station. It is being built in Cambridge Bay, Nunavut, using many local businesses and tradespeople. The location was picked with input from Indigenous peoples in the region. The building will have laboratories and rooms for teaching and training. It will be a modern center to study weather conditions and changes, **greenhouse gases,** wildlife, and pollution levels in the ocean including **microplastics**. With more traffic in the Arctic waterways, satellites help trace weather, the location of ships, and ice floes.

▼ The graves of three of Franklin's crew on Beechey Island. The ice-free water makes it possible for cruise ships to take tourists to the site.

ANALYZE THIS

Now that Arctic waters are ice free for longer each year, more ships can sail through the area. What effects might there be on historic sites such as the graves on Beechey Island? What ways can governments protect them?

A NEW WORLD SEA ROUTE

With rising temperatures and more ice melting, it is not only the faster route that makes the Arctic valuable now. The Arctic has many **natural resources**. The Northwest Passage is a way to access metals such as nickel, iron, and copper. There are also deposits of uranium, natural gas, and oil. The increased use of the Northwest Passage has caused **controversy** over who owns the route. Canada claims that it is a national waterway between its landmasses. The new high Arctic research center, the National Historic sites of the *Terror* and *Erebus,* as well as RCMP and military posts on northern islands, are all ways Canada's government is showing that its boundaries include the Arctic waters around its northern islands.

The United States, Russia, and other countries believe that the Northwest Passage is an international sea route. They think ships should have the right to travel there without restrictions. They do not want Canada blocking their ships. China plans to send cargo ships through the passage because it is shorter than sailing through the Panama Canal. The Law of Sea Convention splits the Arctic among five nations: the United States, Russia, Canada, Denmark, and Norway.

"It is we Inuit that are using the Northwest Passage as an inland waterway that is also surrounded by our settlements. It is a homeland!"

John Amagoalik, elder statesman, Resolute Bay, 2012

ANALYZE THIS

What sources might be useful if you are looking for information on oil drilling in the Arctic. What is the context of Arctic exploration today? What bias might you find? How can you get a balanced view?

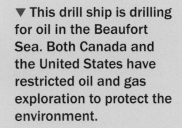

▼ This drill ship is drilling for oil in the Beaufort Sea. Both Canada and the United States have restricted oil and gas exploration to protect the environment.

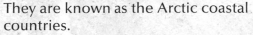

They are known as the Arctic coastal countries.

Indigenous people from the Arctic claim that this area is part of their land. When the sea between islands is frozen over, they use the waterways like highways. They have hunted, fished, and lived in this territory for thousands of years. For centuries they have used an Inuit term, *tallurugik*, to describe this route through the islands. Canadian and International law supports the Inuit's rights to their way of life in the Arctic regions. This includes the sea covered by ice most of the year and the resources both above and below the ice. The United Nations has upheld their rights with the U.N. Declaration on the Rights of Indigenous Peoples. Canada has outlined Indigenous peoples' rights in section 35 of the Constitution Act. The Canadian government is working to share the role of governing the Arctic and the Northwest Passage with Indigenous peoples.

▼ The HMCS *Fredericton* patrols the Arctic waters in Frobisher Bay. The ships are a signal that Canada believes the water in between the islands is within Canadian borders.

TIMELINE

1497 John Cabot, working for King Henry VII, explores the northeastern coast of North America

1576 Martin Frobisher, English seaman, sails as far as the Hudson Strait while searching for a passage to Asia

1611 English explorer Henry Hudson sails into Hudson Bay and James Bay, but is abandoned by his crew and never heard from again

1819 William Edward Parry sails as far west as Melville Island

1825 John Franklin returns to the Arctic. He sails from the Mackenzie River north and stays along the coastline

1845/1846 Franklin and his crews spend the winter on Beechey Island. Three crew members die and are buried there

June 11, 1847 Sir John Franklin dies

1847 Lady Jane Franklin urges the Admiralty to send out a search party

1850 Robert McClure sets out in the *Investigator* to find Franklin. His ship is trapped in ice. He and his crew are rescued by the HMS *Resolute*

1857 Lady Franklin pays for Francis McClintock in the *Fox* to look for her husband

1497

1800

1845

1860

1534 Jacques Cartier of France sails up the St. Lawrence River thinking it is a route to the west

1585 John Davis of England starts the first of three voyages to find and sail the Northwest Passage

1818 John Ross is sent from England. He makes it to Lancaster Sound and believes mountains block the way farther west

1819 John Franklin makes his first journey to the Arctic by land. He travels north of Saskatchewan. He is not well prepared and loses 11 men to injuries and starvation

1845 Sir John Franklin sets sail again for the Arctic on the HMS *Terror*. Captain James Fitzjames commands the HMS *Erebus*

Sept 1846 The *Terror* and *Erebus* become trapped in ice off King William Island

1848 Knowing the expedition had food for only three years, the Admiralty finally sends out a search party for Franklin and his crew

1859 Lieutenant Hobson of McClintock's party finds the stone cairn with the written record inside

1902 Otto Sverdrup explores and names the islands farthest west.

1905 Amundsen completes an east to west route of the Northwest Passage.

June 1940 Henry Larsen is the first Canadian to complete the Northwest Passage. He sailed west to east through the passage in the *St. Roch*.

1984 Dr. Owen Beattie travels to Beechey Island and exhumes members of Franklin's buried crew.

Sept 2014 The HMS *Erebus* is found off King William Island.

Sept 2016 The HMS *Terror* is found in Terror Bay.

1900

2017

1903 Roald Amundsen leaves for the Arctic in his ship the *Gjøa*.

1909 Matthew Henson, the first African-American Arctic explorer, joins Robert Peary in his bid to reach the North Pole.

1954 Canadian Owen Robertson is the first to complete a west to east passage in one year.

2010 Researchers find the wreck of the *Investigator* in Mercy Bay.

Dec 2016 President Obama and Prime Minister Justin Trudeau sign an agreement to protect millions of acres from drilling in the Arctic.

Map of the Northwest Passage

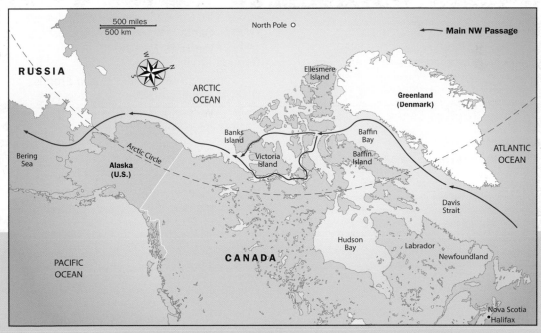

BIBLIOGRAPHY

QUOTATIONS AND IMAGE

Page 4: Collingwood, R. G. *The Idea of History*. Oxford University Press, 1946.

Page 8: Annan, Kofi. Address to the World Bank Conference, June 22, 1997. http://www.un.org/press/en/1997/19970623.sgsm6268.html

Page 10: Town, Stephen R., *The Last Viking: The Life of Roald Amundsen*. Da Capo Press, 2013.

Page 16: José, Francisco Sionil. Transcript of speech, University of Pangasinan, February 11, 2009.

Page 20: Lord Haddington, May 1845, http://bit.ly/2hoTgxH

Page 24: Historic Maps Collection, Department of Rare Books and Special Collections, Princeton University Library.

Page 34: Beattie, Owen. *Cryptic Canada*. Owlkids, 2012. p. 16.

Page 38: National Post online: http://bit.ly/2hoc93L

EXCERPTS

Page 7: http://www.ric.edu/faculty/rpotter/inuittest.html

Page 14: https://books.google.ca/books?id=sJSlOlGJmq8C&printsec=frontcover#v=onepage&q&f=false

Page 20: http://www.canadianmysteries.ca/sites/franklin/voyage/voyagePreparation_en.htm

Page 23: http://bit.ly/2Bb27aG

Page 25: http://www.historymuseum.ca/cmc/exhibitions/hist/frobisher/fr57603e.shtml

Page 26: McClintock, Sir Francis Leopold. *The Voyage of the "Fox'" in the Arctic Seas: In Search of Franklin and His Companions*. Touchwood, 2012.

Page 28: Nansen, Fridtjof. *Farthest North: Vol II* Nabu Press, 2014.

Page 31: http://frammuseum.no/news/fram_museum_news/news_archive_2017/amundsen___s_personal_diary_from_the_northwest_passage_launc

Page 36: https://www.therecord.com/living-story/2616529-uw-anthropologist-joins-search-for-lost-ships-of-franklin/

Page 40: http://arcticjournal.ca/uncategorized/inuit-view-on-canadas-arctic-sovereignty/

TO FIND OUT MORE

NONFICTION

Beattie, Owen and Geiger, John. *Buried in Ice*. Scholastic Publishing, 1992.

Johnson, Dolores. *Onward: A Photobiography of African-American Polar Explorer Matthew Henson*. National Geographic Children's Books, 2006.

Knudsen, Anders. *Sir John Franklin*. Crabtree Publishing, 2007.

Staunton, Ted. *The Dreadful Truth: The Northwest Passage*. Formac Publishing, 2007.

HISTORICAL FICTION

Rogers, Stan. *Northwest Passage*. Groundwood Books, 2013.

Wilson, John. *I Am Canada: Graves of Ice: The Lost Franklin Expedition*. Scholastic Canada, 2014.

DIGITAL COLLECTIONS

Osher Map Library: Smith Center for Cartographic Education.

MULTIMEDIA

Watch footage of the underwater wreck of the HMS *Terror* with the researchers who helped find her: http://bit.ly/2ca28Tf

INTERNET GUIDELINES

Finding good source material on the Internet can sometimes be a challenge. When analyzing how reliable the information is, consider these points:

- Who is the author of the page? Is it an expert in the field or a person who experienced the event?
- Is the site well known and up to date? A page that has not been updated for several years probably has out-of-date information.
- Can you verify the facts with another site? Always double-check information.

- Have you checked all possible sites? Don't just look on the first page a search engine provides. Remember to try government sites and research papers.
- Have you recorded website addresses and names? Keep this data so you can backtrack and verify the information you want to use.

WEBSITES:

Kid-friendly news
Learn all about the discovery of the HMS *Erebus*:
http://teachingkidsnews.com/2014/09/22/2-franklin-expedition/

Voyage through the NW Passage today
Follow along with journalist Elizabeth Kerr on her photo-filled blog as she takes a modern-day trip through the Northwest Passage aboard the *Ocean Endeavor*:
http://bit.ly/2fpvth4

Awesome stories
Discover what the ice mummies on Beechey Island can tell us about Franklin's expedition:
http://bit.ly/1NWKOP4

Osher Map Library
This collection from the Osher Map Library shows how maps of the Arctic slowly became more accurate with each expedition: http://oshermaps.org/exhibitions/arctic-exploration/section-one

Canadian National Archives
Read primary source documents of explorers' journals at the the National Archives site:
http://bit.ly/2wt9r09

GLOSSARY

adopted Started to follow an idea

Allies During World War II, the armed forces of the United States, Canada, Britain, the U.S.S.R, and their related countries

archaeologists People who dig up and study artifacts from historic sites

archive A place where historical documents are kept, or a group of documents themselves

artifacts Objects made by human beings

auditory Related to hearing

bias Prejudice in favor of or against one thing, person, or group. Primary and secondary sources of evidence may show bias.

British Associated with Britain, which comprises England, Scotland, and Wales

cairn A mound of rough stones

cannibalism Eating the flesh of your own species

collaboration Working with others to do something

colonize To set up a colony, which is a settlement in one country governed by people from a different country

commissioned Given the command of a ship

conservators People that protect things from damage or misuse

context Things that influence and are happening during an event that one needs to know to help historical understanding

controversy Disagreement

correspondence Writing letters back and forth

critically Analyzing the good and bad of a subject

culture The ideas, customs, and behaviors of a distinct people

digitally In number code, as used by computers

endurance Able to hold out for a long time

English Associated with England, a part of Great Britain

evaluate To examine and judge the worth of something

evidence A body of facts or information to show whether something is true. Primary and secondary sources are used as evidence.

exhumed Dug up a dead body

exotic Something new and unusual

freight Goods or cargo transported by truck, train, ships, or planes

geographic Referring to landforms

greenhouse gases Gases released into the air from the burning of fossil fuels, in particular coal, oil, and natural gas. Greenhouse gases lead to climate change.

heroics Behavior that is bold and often honored

historian A person who studies evidence from or about a particular time or event that has happened in the past

impassable Cannot travel along or through

Indigenous peoples Original inhabitants of a region or country: used as a general term referring to tribes living in the United States or Canada

interpretation The analysis and explanation of the meaning of evidence

Inuit Indigenous peoples of the Arctic regions

letters patent A document given by a king or queen giving a person certain rights

mainland The main part of a country or territory with islands

microplastics Extremely tiny pieces of plastic in the environment

natural resources Materials in nature that can be used in business or industry

permanent Lasting forever

perspective Point of view

portray To show or represent

preserved Saved in its original condition

primary sources Firsthand memories, accounts, documents, or artifacts from the past that serve as historical records about what happened at a particular time or event

remote Far away from other settlements

scurvy A disease from a lack of vitamin C

secondary sources Evidence of an event usually created some time after it happened; a historian's or artist's interpretations of primary sources

security risk A person or thing that is dangerous to the safety of others

sledge A sled on runners usually pulled by animals

society A group of people forming a single community with its own distinctive culture and institutions

sovereignty The rights of a state or government to govern itself

tertiary sources Evidence of an event usually created some time after it happened, using primary and secondary sources. Tertiary means third in order.

tight-knit Bound together by strong relationships

tragedy A sad event

transcripts Written versions of something spoken or recorded

translation Spoken or written words in a language that is different from the language in which they were created, to give the same meaning

uncharted Not on any map

unique One of a kind

visual Referring to images you can see

vital Extremely important

INDEX